FIX MY TEAM

IDEAS TO HELP TEAM LEADERS
HANDLE THE HEADACHE
OF MESSY TEAMS

NADEEN SIVIC

For more information, email Nadeen@messyteams.com

ISBN: (paperback) 979-8-88759-622-8

ISBN: (ebook) 979-8-88759-623-5

DOWNLOAD THE WORKING TEMPLATES FOR FREE!

Read this first:

To save time and help you find out more about your messy team, I would like to offer you a working version of the templates inside this book, along with lots more additional information about messy teams

I know it can be a daunting and confusing process working with messy teams, and a notebook sometimes just doesn't cut it.

If you'd like an editable copy of the templates and additional information, you can download them at:

MessyTeams.com/Templates

Dedication

To my readers:

If you are young and just starting out in team leadership, then this book is dedicated to you. The information is designed to serve as a catalyst for you to go deeper into the world of leadership. When I was in my twenties, I struggled with the messiness of teams in conflict, and I didn't do particularly well at times, mainly because the resources and knowledge I needed weren't presented to me (the internet wasn't a thing back then). Along the way, I've met many young team leaders in need of help, guidance and mentoring. If that's you, then this book is my dedication to your continued and ongoing evolution.

To my son:

Writing this book sometimes meant we didn't get to hang out as much as we wanted to. I'm sorry. But know that this book is as much a letter to your future self, as it is for my readers today. And even if you don't follow in my footsteps, there are still relevant lessons here on how to be the best person you can be at work, at home and in life overall.

Writing this book was a very difficult task for me. My brain isn't as organised as I want it to be, and my writing is not as advanced or powerful as it could be. I sometimes feel embarrassed that people will laugh at my ideas, because there are a lot of smart people on the planet. Much smarter than me.

But I still did it.

It's important to remember to just do a little bit each day. If you mess it up, say *so what* and keep going. If you get it wrong, learn the lesson and keep going.
Just keep going, ok.
I love you more than chocolate, my little one.

To Alex, the love of my life:

On a daily basis, I forget how different our worlds are, and that I probably seem like some crazy alien woman tapping away at my computer every day. I know you don't get why I love this stuff so much. I barely understand why myself on a good day. But I do.
Thank you for your never-ending supply of love, support and wine.

Contents

Introduction

Before we start, I need to get something out of the way.

What you're about to learn from reading this mini handbook is nothing groundbreaking or revolutionary. Everything I talk about is from theories, models and ideas already formed by people much more intelligent than I am. But they are methods that I've used and drawn from in my daily life, managing tech teams with consistent results.

So why are you reading this?

Because, although the models and theories are not new, they may be new to you, and even if they aren't, you may struggle to understand how to use them in practise.

During my career, I have undertaken a lot of training on how to become a great leader or manager, only to return to work wondering how to use the skills and techniques I've been taught. I found it confusing and frustrating in equal measures. In the relative safety of a classroom, things always seemed to make sense, and I had no trouble shining in any of the role plays or exercises. But in the real world, these simple models soon became complex, complicated and almost impossible to apply.

What looked pretty straightforward during class made no sense to me in the real world and rendered few results. Why? I was using the materials correctly and following the steps. What was going wrong here?

In one scenario, I spent weeks studying how to measure story points and run a burndown chart, and *still* my teams were coming up short of their sprint goals or project milestones.

I felt like I was wasting energy and money on learning. Was it me? Maybe I wasn't as clever as I thought or cut out to be a team leader. Or perhaps I chose the wrong course. Maybe I should have taken a more expensive option to get better tuition and content. It could have been that the training I chose wasn't relevant to the problems I was trying to solve.

It took years of ruminating on this dilemma, while still forging ahead with my own unique, brusque style. I figured if I had two or three like-minded team members on my side, they would pick up the bulk of the work and voilà. Results. It's called the Pareto distribution theory (also known as the 80/20 rule), which is a valid theory, but not a good one for cultivating amazing teams. Considering my inexperience and limited training, it seemed a reasonable approach at the time. And sometimes it worked.

Sometimes.

In my constant search for the perfect solution to making an ideal team, I eventually came to realise the lack of consistent results was because:

1. I was trying to apply a bunch of random models without asking if they were the correct solution for the team and the situation, because,

2. I needed to make more of an effort to understand the underlying root causes of these messy, incongruent teams.

And the underlying root cause of most messy teams is *people*.

Instead of looking at how people associated themselves as individuals into the way of working, and as a group with each other, I was solely focussing on a textbook academic approach, using templates, Excel spreadsheets, projects plans, status reports... *yawn*

Of course, you need plans and objectives for people to focus on and deliver. Particularly when it comes to focussing messy teams. But they are only tools, and in our industry, they can change overnight, depending on the latest and most excellent 'team solutions' from the next tech startup.

I don't know about you, but over the decades, I have witnessed several transformation attempts in large organisations deliver average results. Swathes of high-priced transformation specialists arrive and dock themselves alongside messy teams, and a year later, the results are moderate, and the teams are exhausted.

My evidence is purely observational and anecdotal, but if I were a betting woman, I'd say this is common-place inside corporate companies, and sadly, has nothing to do with the outstanding hard-working consultants doing their best. It is more to do with the focus they have on *process*, and not on people.

You see, processes are a static thing on paper, and can be rewritten at the drop of a hat. In fact, like code, you could write a process ten different ways and get to the same result, eventually.

People, on the other hand, are the complete opposite. They are complex, unpredictable, evolving, unwinding beings that ebb and flow adaptively (or not) to the world they interact with. Even at work. Especially at work.

In the first of my handbook series, I want to show you the things I wish I had learnt when I was starting, in order to help you avoid the frustrations and stresses of fixing and leading messy, dysfunctional teams. You could call this a *letter to my younger self* series, which I hope you will find helpful.

Before you dive in, I don't gild the lily. I try to tell it like it is. I'm about being real first and positive second, because I don't believe there is any point in what I like to coin 'positive, happy clapping'.

To be a great team leader, you need to have a great sense of stoicism and be able to read reality. I hate to say it, but you will mainly be dealing with people on a personal level, not so much their skills level. The harsh reality is that some people will come to work and produce positive, happy outcomes, and others will be mean, judgemental, self-centred and quite destructive to the team's goals. And even worse, they are going to deny they are like that, making your job as a team leader a rather challenging one.

I'm excited that you have joined me, and as we take this journey together, I'd like to offer this mantra that I take into each of my days leading teams:

'Transformation is the empathetic management of your people and how they respond to the change you are asking them to undertake.' – Me, 2022

Let's dive in!

SECTION 1

Preparing for Battle

Congratulations. You've been promoted. Finally, your big break has come. It's day one, and you are about to take your first call on your first day with your new line manager, who has tasked you with the job of fixing a messy team. It was an amazing job offer and to be given the responsibility of sorting out this team after the departure of the previous manager…what a great chance to show the world what you can do.

So. What are you going to do first?

My very first team leader role was User Acceptance Training (UAT) manager on a very large application project in a telecommunications company, where I was put in charge of 10 user test analysts required to validate a business-critical application. The testing domain contained some 300 staff members, and the development and project management office (PMO) was run by IBM GSA. The project took up two entire floors of a 29-storey building in

Melbourne's CBD, and the brief was to get the team into shape, sort out the planning and increase output.

I was 26 years old.

Needless to say, the phrase 'deer trapped in the headlights' was an understatement, and even though I had the *world's most amazing boss and mentor*, I was still a bit lost at times on how to deal with some of the untidiness of it all in the first few months. So, I buried myself in the structure of the processes being given to me via the transformation team and hoped for the best.

I wouldn't say that I was a complete failure, as it won me my next promotion, but what I will say, is that, looking back, it was an enormous responsibility for someone so young, who had zero game plan going in. And I made a lot of mistakes that could have been avoided if I'd had a game plan.

No matter what the situation, good, bad or ugly, you should always have a game plan going in. And by 'game plan', I mean a rinse-and-repeat approach to getting your team from chaos to stable in the shortest possible time. Which is what we are going to learn in this book. I'm going to show you how I approach messy teams and hope it works for you too.

First things first, why are you here?

CHAPTER 1

Greater Expectations

If you sat down in a room and asked your team the questions below, do you think they would give you identical answers?

- What is the reason for the current project?
- Can you name one or two key success factors for the company this year?
- What are the three top pain points that could bring about immediate improvement if changed?
- Who is responsible for making changes in the team to enhance productivity?

Now, ask the management team and senior leadership team the same questions. Do you think you would get the same answers?

We take for granted that we, and others around us, understand the company's direction and are all working to the exact expectations, but this is often not the case. Even the slightest difference of opinion can send people off in different directions, causing friction and disagreement that could have been avoided with better communication.

So before you embark on the journey of fixing a messy team, you need to clarify expectations. There is a saying in corporate, 'Never assume. It makes an ass out of you and me.' Cheeky as this is, it is accurate, and the root cause of many projects going off-piste. Nothing is worse than thinking you have understood the expected outcomes and goals only to get a few months into the journey and find a slight nuance in your thinking has thrown things off course.

It happens to the best of us, and this is why I strongly encourage you to get clear about the expected outcomes before you start. Don't assume that everyone wants 'quicker, faster, cheaper', although they generally do. It is best to let your leadership team determine clear outcomes.

To help put context around the things leadership tends to focus on, I've outlined a few key areas below to help you formulate a set of questions. If you are stuck in pulling a questionnaire together, you can email me for one. Details are in the back of the book.

Typically, the things leadership look for, fall into these broad categories.

Predictable Delivery

Of all the processes and activities we undertake in technology, nothing causes us more grief than estimating. This is because, although the team might have lots of experience with an application or technology, every new project will be unique and uncharted territory. Hence, the ambiguity in timelines.

Small pieces of work are easy to estimate; time horizons are easy to realise when they are close. Bigger pieces of work, not so much.

On one side, you have the team doing the work, who sometimes give an educated guess. On the other side is management, who are responsible for getting a return on the fixed budget and understandably panic a bit when timelines run over.

When will it be done?

An important thing to note here is that they may not be talking about *fast* delivery. In the modern, agile world of technology, speed to market is often assumed as a key driver, but that isn't always the case. Predictable delivery may be more important than fast delivery.

Being predictable means feeling confident about a future event occurring. For some companies, this may mean quarterly. For others, it may mean twice a year. Predictable delivery is essential, because there will be other parts to the project, such as sales, marketing and training, that need coordinating around the completion of certain milestones.

Improve the Quality

Everyone wants to improve quality of technology products. Production defects are annoying and costly, both in terms of impact on future work (think constant hotfixes and interruptions) or the brand's image. But do they need perfection?

I've always found this question of quality interesting, because the word 'quality' can mean different things to different people, depending on where they are in the food chain. To a test manager, quality means few to no defects. To a sales guy, quality might mean a beautifully presented product that sells itself and blows the competition out of the water.

Ask the questions and find out what a high-quality offering looks like in that new market space. Is it the number of defects that get raised after each implementation, or is it that they want the user interface to keep up with modern trends?

Costs

The biggie. It is without doubt that a healthy balance sheet is one where costs are lower than revenue. Everybody wants to lower costs, but this is quite a difficult one to achieve in the short term, and there's no guarantee that getting a messy team on the straight and narrow will decrease costs.

There are too many variables in this one. If this becomes a focus area, it's best to ask why they believe their development costs are too high. For example, do they have test teams sitting around for six months because the development kept running over time? Or perhaps their deployment method is too manual and takes two people days or weeks to migrate and implement, rather than one person pressing a few buttons to spin up an environment and migrate some data.

Technology leadership teams often fall prey to an 'assembly-line' mentality, believing teams should be seamlessly handing over work from one set of hands to another, like cars on an assembly line. It's my opinion that this has come about from the misuse of the 'waterfall method'.

The waterfall method is a linear process that moves from one group to another in a sequential line. Like a car manufacturing plant, which is fine when you are building the same thing each time. But technology doesn't create the same thing each time. It solves unique problems for a set of users, so the work pattern is different, and there will always be a lag in the process.

And perhaps that is true, but if the overall cadence of their work programme sees a lot of projects overlapping, then you can hardly expect one or two product analysts to produce functional specifications for five interrelated projects in the same month.

The point is that cost reduction is complex and not something you can guarantee at a local level. If you find yourself in a conversation about reducing costs, my advice is to clarify what they mean and explain the difficulties in meeting targets. Be careful not to commit yourself to cost-reducing initiatives.

Innovate Quicker

Everyone wants to get to market faster than their competitors. Getting things to market means quicker feedback. It may not mean quicker return on investment (ROI). Perhaps the product is a flop, but it means you learnt from that flop failure faster and can now pivot quickly without having wasted millions on unsellable products. Having the ability to ship a product earlier, in smaller iterations, and testing the market, is smart.

Companies that don't deliver, or discuss delivering, innovative products and services, find it difficult to stay competitive. And not just in their products but their leadership and teams. The creative mindset has become a big part of the cultural shift as we move deeper into the 21st century, and it isn't going anywhere soon.

How does this relate to fixing a messy team? Well, it isn't directly related, and to be honest, like costs, this is something that you can't immediately deliver as part of your journey with the team. As your team starts to straighten itself out and matures towards a competent delivery model, individuals in your team may surface, who show innovative talent. At that stage, you can start the conversations with the leadership team on how to implement an innovation culture inside the workplace. For this reason, innovation should be considered a secondary initiative.

But that is not in the scope of this book.

So once you have your expectations conversation laid out, have collated that information and confirmed with your boss, you need to have the following discussion before you go into battle.

People

People can be a sticky topic in the corporate world, primarily because of the apparent complexities. However, this is a big part of becoming an expert in tidying up messy teams. If you already have degrees in behavioural psychology, you're ahead of me. If you don't, it's not a problem. There are things you can learn, and we will do that in this book.

It's funny. I've been approached to sort out processes, figure out the best way to test a complex system, get the developers and vendors integrated into a plan or get teams to deliver faster – or just deliver! But I've never been tasked with improving the team's *people*. Having spent three years as a corporate trainer, I know it's because leadership believes it is the job of the training department. But the type of training given to people in tech teams oftentimes doesn't address these sorts of issues. And ultimately, it's the team leader's job to create an amazing team.

I work from the premise that, to fix a seriously dysfunctional team, you have to start with the people first. If the COVID-19 pandemic taught us nothing else, it's that, if you take the people out of the equation, all you have is a bunch of empty buildings full of desks and papers.

Your objective?

In the infant stages of your journey with a chaotic team, your goal is to get them *stable*, so they can focus on their daily tasks systematically. It means you'll concentrate on understanding where they are as a group, how they interact, what's causing the friction that makes things so complicated and where you can insert little improvements or quick wins, to gently bring them together as one cohesive unit.

Key Takeaway: Expectations can differ greatly depending on your perspective. What you may see as the priority to fix, your boss may see differently, depending on his or her objectives. Getting clear about what matters before you head down the rabbit hole is always a good idea.

There are many things that might need to be addressed in your team. The main thing to note is that the impact you can make alone, as a team leader, will be limited. It will also take time, the amount of which can be difficult to assess until the extent of the issues are truly uncovered.

Therefore, your best approach is to focus on providing predictable delivery and improving team morale.

Let's start by understanding a little bit about team morale, group dynamics and learning how to recognise a team in trouble.

CHAPTER 2

Observation

Power struggles; conflict; apathy; lack of clarity; no vision; bad communication, or worse, *no* communication; friction and conflict; passive-aggressive behaviour; backstabbing and arguments; selfish ladder-climbing at the cost of team outcomes; no commitment to plans; waffly discussions; non-inclusion; and clandestine sabotaging behaviour.

What the…?

It's what psychologist Bruce W. Tuckman calls the 'storming' phase. It's part of a fluid cycle that explains the relationships and behavioural outcomes a group experiences at work and the impacts of either negative or positive behaviours on a group's value results as a team.

If you are unfamiliar with Tuckman's Model of Group Development, I highly recommend you start reading *anything* on this topic you can get your hands on, as this model can be a valuable barometer for a team's health check at every step.

As you go through the journey, you won't only be using correct processes to ensure the work gets done; you will be using Tuckman's model to identify where the group is at and how serious their non-cohesion is overall.

Why is understanding this model so important?

Explaining Tuckman's Group Development

In 1956, psychological researcher Bruce W. Tuckman published findings on work he was doing in the theory of group dynamics and theorised his idea that all groups go through a series of stages in order to face challenges, tackle problems, find solutions, plan out the work, then deliver the results. He determined that there were four distinct phases: Forming – Storming – Norming – Performing. To note, there is a newly introduced fifth phase called Adjourning, which involves the standing down of a team once the work is completed. This tends to apply to project-based work, where there is a set outcome, and the team are no longer needed. As this book is targeted specifically at teams that are ongoing and long-term, I've decided to omit this phase.

How each group moved through these phases depended on several variables considered unique to the group and focussed on the interpersonal relationship between the group members and, in the case of work teams, the inclusion of certain things inside the organisation.

Forming

During this initial phase, the group comes together to explore an opportunity to address a challenge or problem. This is where individuals are assessing the landscape of 'who's who' in the team. Introverts may choose to observe, rather than contribute, as a way of assessing the playing field, whereas extroverts will be verbal, open and forge ahead, trying to take the lead.

This is a phase of testing. Individuals are learning to interact with each other at this stage, and as this learning progresses through daily interactions, the empathetic team members will adapt the way they approach communication and problem-solving to find a good fit. Unempathetic members will oftentimes refuse to adapt to the evolving formation, causing small niggles and friction to arise.

During formation, team members tend to be more polite and frequently tread lightly until they have figured each other out. This politeness may get in the way of providing the best solutions, and so you need to be mindful of this and coax out deeper conversation where you feel necessary.

People tend to be excited when a new project starts, as they see themselves in a position of newness, where there is a chance to get things right this time. As the new team is formed, hope will fuel their behaviours towards initial politeness and tolerance, alongside higher levels of patience and a desire to help each other.

The forming phase is often when a project is kicked off and aligns with the early stages of planning and requirements mapping. But it can also occur when a team loses one or more members and new individuals are introduced into the group.

Often, projects that fail, or teams that go to war can be traced back to:

1. No clear mission statement being understood and agreed upon from the outset.
2. Assumptions about ways of working. While some may understand their role and the swim lane they occupy, they may make incorrect assumptions about the functions of other team members, leading to misunderstanding and, ultimately, missed milestones.

A system of values, and a clear understanding of the mission, are two things that every team should have. Values are oftentimes overlooked at team level, but without them, conflict arises very quickly. Especially where you have diverse opinion.

To explain, diversity in a team is often a good thing, because those different points of view will ultimately benefit the end product. But when people don't see the merit in our ideas, this can feel like a very personal attack for some people. Especially those who pride themselves on the pursuit of learning, knowledge and creativity.

We definitely want to promote diversity of input in a team, but there has to be an overriding system of values that holds it all together.

As the project progresses, these misunderstandings can compound themselves and trickle down, causing significant disruption and upheaval in both the plan and the team. The result can end in the team entering the storming phase. This is something to be avoided.

These are the typical characteristics you will observe during the forming phase:

- The avoidance of controversy and a higher level of politeness
- A hesitance to be direct in challenging ideas
- Discussions about things not on-topic
- The need for safety, resulting in looking for constant approval to do things

In general, there is a strong desire to please each other, get along and avoid conflict.

During the forming stage, there are certain things you can do to bring about some stability. They are:

Create a team charter. If done right, they are very useful for uncovering what people really think they are at work to do.

Establish specific short-term objectives, and if they don't have any, create or adjust the project plan. If they work in an agile environment, redesign the plan, so they are working toward short-term goals with a three-month horizon.

Identify the roles and responsibilities of team members as individuals and provide a view of how those roles fit together.

Establish team ground rules using a team working agreement. The charter speaks to the higher level and focuses on values. On the other hand, team working agreements are transitory, because they focus on a project and the details behind how the team will operate. For example, meetings can be no more than 15 minutes with four people, or no meetings before 9 a.m.

Approach this with an open mind and the intention of discovery. Doing it as a group first is often ideal. Then, approach individuals to confirm anything you feel needs more clarification. Understanding their expectations will give you a view of the individual's belief system concerning where they sit in the team and the responsibilities they need to undertake. You will quickly understand who is a team player and who is not.

Storming

As the work progresses and the group starts to dance around each other in getting their tasks underway, things, such as politics and culture, begin to rise to the surface. At this stage, the members may oppose the way each other works, or they may not agree on specific ways of working.

Tolerance levels for differences in opinion, approaches to work, or personality can bubble up, and conflicts begin to arise. In his studies, Tuckman discovered that only 50% of groups go through this phase, so it's not a given that all teams end up in a dogfight over a biscuit. But it is still essential to understand this phase, as it is a) the most destructive to team performance and b) the toughest to resolve.

You may witness things like:

- Disagreements that remain unresolved
- Plodding progress or a lack of any progress at all
- Confusion and apathy causing a lack of momentum
- Individuality, a reluctance to share work
- Invisible team members or side-lined team members
- Vying for leadership and seeking the spotlight from senior management
- Feelings of defensiveness from some members

A storming team is usually underpinned by power struggles between senior members, contending for attention and control, while the less vocal members become unheard. Junior members frequently become collateral damage in team warfare and retreat to their corners, contributing little.

This phase tends to result in less-than-ideal outcomes and late deliveries, as people refuse to agree on how to create as a cohesive group. Instead, they will put personal opinions and egos ahead of the team goal, and oftentimes become more attached to the work and their own opinions. Then, momentum suffers. This phase is the reason I wrote this book.

Fundamentally, the storming phase is the most destructive of the phases, and generally, it's because of conflict. And I'm not talking about the healthy kind of conflict. I'm talking about the 'I'm right, and you're wrong' sort of conflict that comes from attention-seeking individuals and a need for personal validation, more than the desire to find solutions that are best for the company.

It's easy to write this friction off as being 'personality clashes', but storming can go deeper than this. Of all the challenges you'll face in your career, understanding the drivers and motivations of people and using them to create a productive, performant team is going to be the biggest, and never-ending, challenge.

So what can you do to address this in these infant stages of the process?

You'll need to figure out things like:

- Inter- and intra-personal relationships, along with unique differences. This will involve understanding how they operate as individuals. Hence, why the team charter and team working agreements are pivotal to getting out of the storming phase.
- How to address conflict. Your conflict resolution skills will be pushed to their limits as you establish ground rules and reset team roles.
- How to address breaches against the team working agreement. Not addressing this will break trust and confidence in your ability to lead the team.
- What motivates team members. Some members will need support, some members will need praise, and some will need to move on to a different opportunity. Figuring out which you need to apply is going to be the biggest challenge of them all, because it means figuring out the people and their motivations. Sounds simple but takes a lifetime to master.

The key to getting people out of this phase is to build intra-team relationships and reinforce a system of values designed to produce a happy, healthy team.

A lot of leaders hate the storming phase and don't really know how to approach it. Some take a very HR approach by reiterating role cards and reminding people of their contractual employment responsibilities. Some leaders choose to work solely on fixing the process, in the hope everyone will follow it, and things will be magically resolved. While there is nothing wrong with these approaches, they may not be the right approaches, depending on what the underlying issues are.

Be aware that, while the personal satisfaction level of resolving the storming team is very high, it takes much work and requires enormous levels of self-management and self-care. There will be days when you'll be tearing your hair out at what people do and say. The backlash you get from team members, either direct or indirect, will be very difficult to deal with. And there is no guarantee that you will make it out alive. (I don't mean that literally, of course.) But it would be best if you are prepared for this phase and learn how to understand what is driving the team members to tweak your strategy and win.

In the back of this book, there is a recommended reading list to help. If you are serious about becoming an expert at getting teams out of this storming phase, you should learn everything you can about people. Processes alone will rarely fix the problems, and your ability to lead them out of the storm will depend on how well you can influence them. And that means understanding who they are and why they come to work.

Norming

As the group climatises to the new project work and the individuals become accustomed to each other's personality quirks, they figure out how to communicate democratically, and things start to settle down.

In this phase, team members are open to difficult conversations and don't view conflict as a negative thing, but more as a chance to uncover all the unknowns and address them quickly. If they have been through a storming phase and managed to sort out their differences, you'll find the comradery much better and their alignment tighter. They will become more tolerant of others and put aside judgement to deliver the goals.

When a team enters norming phase, you will feel a shift. They will seem happier, be more open and be willing to cooperate to get a job done. There may be wobbles here and there, but they will work through it with a bit of guidance.

You will generally feel a more pleasant atmosphere and no longer dread approaching the day. It will help if you note this feeling, as it will become your guide. Whenever you find yourself experiencing the feelings that arose during the storming phase, you should take note and start assessing what has caused it. Then seek to fix it quickly.

The norming phase is characterised by the following:

- Repetition of procedures that produce consistent results.
- Continual cadence, without much need for guidance.
- Team dynamics becoming more settled as they prioritise the goal of outcomes over their own needs.
- Less individuality, although it may still occur in individuals for different reasons.
- More self-management by team members, but they will still require some team leadership.
- Team members seeking to solve problems themselves before asking for your help.

When you get to this phase, it will feel like breathing a giant sigh of relief. It doesn't mean the team won't go back to storming; they may. You need to keep your eyes peeled and your senses alert to any outside threats that may disrupt the new harmony.

Be especially prudent about bringing in new team members at this point. It might be unavoidable, because losing people is typical when you try to bring them out of storming. Be mindful of hiring new team members and focus on how they will fit with the team. You should know your team well enough to make sound decisions at this stage. You should try to include them in the process.

Be aware, with new team members, the team may exhibit some forming-type characteristics while the new member settles in. But if they were moving into norming, it shouldn't last too long, and they should keep producing a stable output of work.

Performing

Performing is where the team will take off, and you can step back and assume a guidance role. In fact, at this point, your job as a specialist team leader is more or less done. It doesn't mean you are out of a job – that depends on your chosen career strategy – it just means that you have achieved that sought-after goal of fixing a messy team.

Now you will see personality clashes put aside for the greater good, as they seek to build a plan based on each other's capabilities. During the *norming* phase, you, as the team leader, will tend to drive competency-based planning. This means you will build the plans and assign tasks to the person with the best skills fit. During *performing*, they can figure it out themselves.

They will be more cognizant of potential blockers and seek to resolve things as a group, rather than clamour for the spotlight or compete for management attention, because team members will have come to learn that the sum is greater that its parts. One team, one direction.

Their focus will be on the actual work and doing what they can to achieve the end goal. You should start to see them perform together as a well-oiled machine. They will foresee issues, head off disasters at the pass, be happy to help each other, and continually work to the mantra 'What's the best I can do today to help the team and my company win?'

A performing team will typically look like this:

- A happy, healthy team that requires minimal direction and can be trusted to get the job done.
- When a storm hits, they know what to do and how to resolve it.
- They are fully prepared for any meeting or day they approach and have a solid understanding of what they will achieve in the short and long term.
- They are not afraid to speak up when things affect or impact the status quo and can do it without insult or blame.
- They seek to understand first before taking action.

In an ideal world, a fabulous team will spend a small amount of time in forming, skip through to norming for a second, then fly on into performing mode until the completion of the goal.

Of course, we don't live in an ideal world. And if you are reading this book, it means that you have a team that is either in storming, or keeps slipping into storming every time a new project starts. Using this model to identify your group's development will add a fantastic feather to your cap as far as skills go. Diagnosing where a team is at gives you incredible power, because you aren't running blind.

There are a hundred different ways messy teams come about, and figuring that out is part of the challenge. It is a challenge that can be fun, tiring, frustrating and rewarding all at the same time.

There is a bit of a 'gotcha' about Tuckman's model, and that is just that…it's a *model*. Teams, however, are living, breathing things that can change at the drop of a hat for no apparent reason. One day you are all happily sailing along, and you, as the leader, will feel great, knowing you are coming out of storming into norming, and then *bam*. Someone pulls the rug out from under you.

The phases do not happen sequentially, and just because you've reached performing doesn't mean your work is done. People, business, economic downturns, company restructuring and company growth all play a part in the dynamics of a team.

The first phase of forming may seem to apply only to a newly created team, but that is only partially true. If the basics, like team charters and annual planning, are not in place, a team may operate in forming mode for longer than desired, stopping them from becoming a cohesive group. Likewise, a performing team, through external forces or company restructuring, will often shift back to forming, and possibly even storming, for a while.

Remember, people are the sum total of all their experiences since birth, making us highly complicated creatures. So it stands to reason that a group of individuals together makes the complexity somewhat overwhelming.

Here are some examples to help you think about why a team could take a step back into storming:

- A member resigns. Especially if that person was well-liked and brought a certain positive atmosphere to the table daily, this can be quite shocking to good teams, almost like a breakup.
- You hired a new member only to find their real personality is abrasive, and as a result, they clash with the team.
- Personal problems that cause heavy stress and are manifesting themselves in strange ways.
- People outside the team trying to bypass process, directly approaching team members to influence them into doing things that put the team's goals at risk.
- Someone suddenly puts their owns needs ahead of the team, looking for a promotion or pay rise.

How Do I Use This?

Now that you have some knowledge about group development, we should talk about how to use it in practice. Clearly, the objective is to get your team to at least the norming phase, or better, the performing phase for a time. To help you, I've created a template called 'Where Is My Team?' as a quick reference guide to help you figure out where your team are and what you should consider doing to help them along to a preferred state. You will find this at the end of the book in the section titled Additional Information.

Your powers of observation and critical analysis will be essential if you are to understand why your team is at war. We will discuss 'observation' in Section 2 when assessing your team and applying quick wins. For now, I encourage you to learn as much as possible about Tuckman's Model of Group Development and understand all of the key activities to help move your team to the correct phase.

Key Takeaway: Different situations call for different things. The world is not static, nor is it linear. It is a paradox, and it contradicts itself all the time. Why? Because people contradict themselves all the time. Half the time, they don't even know they are doing it. It's subconscious, and it's nuanced.

Your job is not to become a 'great' team leader but to become an intelligent one. And an intelligent team leader is one who accepts the ambiguity of the contradictory world we operate within. If you are looking for simplicity, where everything fits in a box, and everything aligns to a narrative, I'm afraid you will be in for a bumpy ride. Every day is going to throw you complexities that don't align to the plan, and you're going to have to take what you know and figure it out. Sometimes as you go along.

The top skill to acquire in your job, as well as in life, is the ability to conquer your thoughts and expectations about the world and come to terms with its ever-changing landscape.

If you need everything to be clear, simple and defined in one 'black-and-white' dimension, your job as a team leader is probably going to drive you to a nervous breakdown. You need to learn to operate at ground level *and* 30,000 feet simultaneously. And at the same time, be comfortable in navigating the team's paradoxes so that you can solve complex problems.

And messy teams are complex problems to solve.

CHAPTER 3

The Importance of Team Morale

When a team has existed in the storming phase for some time, their morale will inevitably be low, especially if there has been long-standing conflict and friction. This can result in various things, depending on the team dynamics. Perhaps this team has two or three dominant players who battle it out in every meeting, while the rest stay firmly installed in silence, scared to say anything lest they are shot down in flames. Sound familiar?

Or perhaps there are too many juniors on the team compared to experienced seniors, and resentment has set in, creating a caustic atmosphere.

There are a hundred different ways messy teams come about, and figuring that out is part of the challenge. It is a challenge that can be fun, tiring, frustrating and rewarding all at the same time.

The key focus of this challenge is how to create and maintain morale.

> morale
>
> /məˈrɑːl/
>
> *Noun*
>
> the confidence, enthusiasm, and discipline of a person or group at a particular time.
> "the team's morale was high"

I personally think team morale is linked to one essential thing: how people are treated at work by the leaders and management.

Simple, right? Not really. The key is in defining the word 'treated'. It takes more to maintain team morale than being polite and friendly at work, which should go without saying. But you also have to consider the atmosphere you are creating and whether people will respond positively.

These are the things individuals (often unconsciously) use to determine the state of their morale:

- Do I feel trusted? Am I given agency and autonomy over my work, or is it dictated?
- Are they listening to me? Do they consider my opinion, and is my input and what I do valuable?
- Are we all treated equally, and is there fairness? Is there a good level of inclusiveness?

Of course, it is essential to set goals, create plans, and help the team understand why the goals are important, but when it comes down to it, none of this stuff matters if there is an underlying sense of mistrust or that some people are favoured over others.

Charles Feltman, author of *The Thin Book of Trust*, defines trust in the most eloquent way.

'Trust is choosing to make something important to you vulnerable to the actions of someone else.'

Trust is the basis for every single interaction you have in life. At work, at home, at the cinema, at the supermarket and online. Every interaction, everywhere. The success of your interactions depends heavily on the level of trust you feel. And the level of trust you experience depends on how safe you feel.

It seems a bit woo-woo, right? But at work, this stuff tends to be quite subliminal, happens in nanoseconds and is sometimes difficult to understand. Trust at work isn't something that involves grand and obvious gestures. More often, it's the combination of small things.

Trust is what makes people want to come to work, and I think it's what turns a 'job to pay the rent' into a 'vocation'. Where there is trust, humans thrive, and in my experience, teams that operate in an atmosphere of trust will go above and beyond, not because they *have to* but because they *want to*.

The reason trust makes humans feel *safe*, is because trust stems from *connection*.

Connection is an overlooked thing at work and also a little misunderstood. When I talk about connection, I'm not suggesting that you start a personal relationship with a co-worker beyond what you feel comfortable with. I do tend to think that work is work at the end of the day, but there has to be some kind of affinity that connects you on a human level beyond the tasks of the day.

When that kind of connection grows in your team, you will discover a loyalty that will drive people to protect each other. As team connection takes place, team members will start to pick up the slack when someone is ill or defend another person inside conflict who is being unfairly victimised. This sort of connection is what compels a person to pick up the phone after a daily stand-up meeting and say, 'Hey, I see you're struggling a bit with this thing. Can I help?'

Once this starts to happen, you should see trust grow, and you should start to see your team working more closely together. But when there is no connection, they will be at odds with each other all the time, and you'll witness things like:

- Throwing each other under the bus when things go wrong.
- Public humiliation for asking perceived 'silly questions'.

- Silence and a fear of speaking up as a result of the first two points.
- Individualism.

When you witness an individual team member focussed solely on their own daily tasks, ignoring the plea for help from others, so that they may look good in front of management for completing work on time, and in accordance with the perfect process, you know you have a major issue on your hands. Nothing destroys a team quicker than insular individuality, and it's this sort of thing you want to watch out for, because it a) destroys the concept of team and b) eradicates connection and trust.

Nobody gets up in the morning and thinks to themselves, 'Oh, fantastic. I can't wait to get out there and be made to feel like crap about myself.'

And this is why team morale should be your number one priority, above all else. People come to work to feel like they are part of something, no matter how big or small the role, and they come to work to feel good about themselves. And not just as a valued member of the team but as a human being trying to navigate this thing called life.

The relationship you have with your team is a very personal one, because a successful team is propelled forward by connection. The traditional narrative regarding work is to keep the lines professional, and I agree with that to some extent. I'm not talking about creating the kind of relationships you have at home with your family, but about creating a connection inside the boundaries of the job that tells them they are safe.

A great example is when I build delivery plans and provide management the 'when will it be done milestone'. I do it based on not *just* the people's capacity, but also their *capability*.

At one job, I came across a project manager who proudly presented me with a roadmap with a resource plan that I knew wasn't achievable. After pointing out that he had created a plan on the 'all resources are equal' principle, and that he only had one developer in a team of five who knew the product, he said, 'Oh, I never thought of it like that.'

He had been in the job for over six months and still didn't know the team as individuals to enable better planning. It isn't groundbreaking stuff here; it's common sense. You don't build a plan that has aggressive delivery dates with a team of newbies.

Sadly, as time went on, and I got to know this team leader better, I discovered the reason he didn't know was because he genuinely didn't care to figure it out. He came to work with the solemn belief that you give someone a task and it's their job to get it done. Simple. And when they didn't, he took every opportunity behind the scenes to berate and belittle their existence in the company.

It didn't take long for me to realise he was trying to 'manage up'. Essentially, he was more interested in displaying *his* achievements in front of senior leadership than he was in learning how to be an intelligent team leader to produce a fantastically performant team. Eventually, this led to his demise, because he was a terrible team leader.

CHAPTER 4

Counterfeit Trust

I want to talk for a minute about the concept of counterfeit trust. It is something that I witnessed a lot over the years, and I've no doubt you will run into it as well. So what is it? It is essentially where a team leader implements what they believe to be a great thing for the group, but because they didn't think too hard about what the outcome would be, it ends up doing the opposite. The best way I can explain it is to use an example.

It's quite trendy nowadays to foster open environments, where people are brave enough to call out behaviours they feel are detrimental to the team. Which is fine, because you definitely want a team who feels comfortable raising issues.

These issues may be things like:

- We didn't write a fully aligned plan and lost a week because we had to wait.
- We could have used an additional testing environment.

- We didn't factor in contingency for illness during
  flu season.

But for some reason, I don't know why, parts of our
industry have interpreted the idea of an open environment
to mean one which enables individuals to publicly call out
others for anything, at any time, in the name of team spirit.
This is what the agile methodology calls a 'self-regulating
team', which, in some respects, is a necessary part of team
formation.

But as the team leader, it's your job to keep a close eye on
these things, because not everyone in your team are capable
of delivering critical feedback or challenge with empathy.
I've witnessed teams go from perfectly functional to with-
drawn in the space of a few seconds as a result of a care-
lessly delivered feedback in the spirit of 'team openness'.

The problem with the idea of an open, self-regulated
team is one of human nature. Most of us drift through our
days without much thought to the impact our words have
on others, and when you are in the mosh pit of solving
seriously complex problems, all sorts of egos start emerging
that can cause hurt, anger and confusion inside your team.

Before you start implementing these sorts of textbook
ideas, it's important to consider the personality types you
have in the team and how they will respond. To be clear, I
am not suggesting for a second that you abolish the idea of
openness in your team, but there is a time and a place for
it. Not every decision needs a democratic vote. You should

look to encourage openness with regards to the solutions they come up with during the course of delivering a project, and leave the critique on personalities to more experienced people.

Personality is complex, but understanding the basics and determining where your team fits should be enough to steer you in the right direction when implementing changes like the one we're discussing here. I have made the intentional decision in this book not to delve into the Big 5 and the DISC personality framework, as it really deserves a book of its own. I'd encourage you to take note of these two things, and do some research on the topic. A good place to start is with DISC, sometimes known as DISA. If, like me, you are not into overly academic text, which means you have yellow tendencies, then *Surrounded by Idiots* by Thomas Erikson is the best place to start. What are yellow tendencies? Read his book and you'll see.

Apologies, I digress. Back to our example on counterfeit trust.

Let me give a real-life example that I had to deal with in more recent times.

I once had a developer quit his job because he didn't like the fact that he couldn't call out people in my team on things. The place he had worked before was open and honest, and as he went on to describe it, I felt horrified. What he was suggesting was attacking a team member's *personality*, rather than keeping it impersonal and focussing on work output.

Full transparency, the individual he was complaining about was quite difficult at times in the way he communicated. It was rarely to the point and always around the houses, which the other members of the team found frustrating for two reasons: 1) he was usually right, but 2) he seemed to take pleasure in hearing his own prose and slowing the team down to meet his expectations. You know the type. But, at the end of the day, he was respectful, helpful and a valued member of the team.

To say I was a taken aback by the lack of insight and empathy at the suggestion of being able to call this sort of thing out, would be an understatement.

You want me to create an environment where it is okay for you to publicly call out someone's personality and individuality, which was formed over the entirety *of their lives, from their unique experiences, because you lack the tolerance and patience to interact with someone different from you?*

…is what I wanted to say. But I didn't. Had I done so, I would have been consciously creating an environment where the team would naturally slide into the storming phase, one action at a time, for the sake of one intolerant individual.

Considering this example, you can see how risky it can be to promote a fully open environment. The resigning team member may have been correct in what he was saying, but he lacked the skills on how to stoically regulate himself, given the situation he found himself in, and rather, looked to implement what I deem a trendy approach to team management. Had I done what he asked and implemented such an environment, the team would have collapsed back into chaos. I had set about to create a psychologically safe environment, which previously didn't exist, and for my money, you cannot create a safe working place whilst encouraging a culture where people publicly call out each other in such personal way.

The other problem I faced was, this team member believed it was okay for him to determine the ecosystem and culture of the team. I don't necessarily agree with that. Whilst it is important for team members to provide input and suggestions, ultimately, the team leader is responsible for culture and ecosystem.

In an interview you can find on YouTube https://www.youtube.com/watch?v=W8RmWPqBiBo, Jeff Weiner used a baseball analogy to describe the difference between the role of the manager and the role of the team member. Whilst I'm not a fan of sports analogies, per se, I think this one particularly poignant.

He starts by describing the situation of the pitcher, who is throwing perfectly every time. After a while, the pitcher becomes tired and performance drops. The manager, worried about team performance, approaches the pitcher to discuss the situation, whereupon the pitcher assures the manager he is 'fine, fine, perfect, it's all good.'

The manager returns to the dugout, and the pitcher gives away a home run.

The problem here is that it isn't the pitcher's job to decide whether he is good enough to stay in the game, because that means the pitcher is now deciding the game for the entire team. It's the *manager's* job, for the overall good of the team, to decide whether the pitcher stays in the game or sits on the bench. In this scenario, the pitcher is putting his own needs, his ego and pride, ahead of the group.

There are a few lessons to be taken from this analogy, but the key lesson for me is that it is the team leader's job to determine what is best for the overall team, in order to produce the necessary outcomes. It's a very important differentiation to make as, far too often, new team leaders become more involved with keeping *individuals* happy than focussing on the group as a whole, only to end up with a non-cohesive and messy team.

In the case of my departing developer, I didn't fight at all to keep him, as I had no intention of ever creating the environment he was suggesting, and so he was never going to be happy.

So I acknowledged his feelings on the subject and agreed that the person in question was not straightforward to deal with, but it was a conflict of personality and personal values, rather than a dereliction of duties.

As the leader, you must carefully assess what to do when facing these situations. Seemingly innocent ideas, with the best of intentions, can often backfire if you don't analyse what the outcomes will be in the bigger context of your team and mission.

Key Takeaway: Building and maintaining team morale is very complex, especially if you don't keep your wits about you and use good critical thinking when 'good ideas' come your way.

CHAPTER 5

The Murky World of Unethical Behaviour at Work

Imagine you are at work. Your boss congratulates someone on the success of an important piece of work they worked on, but that you were responsible for initiating, and that you did the heavy lifting to get off the ground.

Now imagine that the person says, 'Thanks, yes, I worked on that' *without* correcting your boss to tell her that, actually, they did *work* on it, but it wasn't all their *own* work. It belonged to someone else, who initiated the project and got the lion's share done. They were only a bit player.

I don't know many people who would feel happy under those circumstances, and neither should they. A person of strong ethics would point out the truth, rather than create an illusion based on an omission.

In my experience, I've discovered that, at the core of discontent, friction between team members can often-times be traced to questionable ethics at work. If you are yet to witness these things inside your team, consider it a huge bonus and one less thing to deal with. However, since it is human nature to bend the truth when it benefits our advancement, learning a bit about ethics at work will immensely help your career as a team transformer.

So, what are ethics exactly?

The study of ethics is one philosophy that analyses the moral conduct that guides either behaviour or a set of activities. In a sense, they are like the core values you choose to live by, or do business by, and are linked to your character. When it comes to questionable behaviour, ethics guide individuals at work concerning what they will and won't accept.

Sidebar: *Personality* is the behavioural patterns you may see in a person that contribute to their uniqueness. Things, such as being outgoing, speaking animatedly, or having a quiet and retrospective disposition, are all traits that belong to personality. *Character* is the deep-seated values a person lives by, like a moral compass.

It will help if you read more on this subject, because, since messy teams come down to unwanted behaviours, knowing the difference between personality and character will steer you in decision-making. What I mean by this is, you don't want to make the mistake of moving someone out of the team because they have an annoying personality, under the illusion that they are 'disruptive', all the while leaving someone else in situ who has questionable character and is lying at every turn to advance their own career.

Ethics is a complicated and expansive philosophy that, in this context, is used to ensure people behave correctly when conducting business. It is a philosophy that dates back to the times of Aristotle and attempts to systemise and seeks to define the concept of right or wrongdoing, justice or injustice, good or evil. Deep stuff, right? It is. And in some respects, I think, understanding ethics and morale theory will make you a better team leader in the long run, as it will help guide your decision-making with individual team members who may not be playing so nice with the others.

We're going to look at applied ethics, specifically business ethics.

Business ethics, or organisational ethics, can be divided into two general areas: external or internal. The types of things *businesses* do to breach ethical boundaries are called *external* ethics. The best examples of this in modern times are Boeing getting caught for corporate espionage, Enron's creative accounting practices to improve its share price position, Napster with its digital copyright infringement, and Xerox for overindulging its revenue figures.

Internal organisational ethics looks at behaviours exhibited by *employees*, either by themselves or to other employees. In researching on the internet, I came across a superb academic paper called 'An Introduction to Organizational Communication', and, in Chapter 2, the author speaks to the question of ethics inside the organisation and what is considered unethical behaviour. Unfortunately, the portal

I found this information on stated that the author wished to remain anonymous, so I cannot attribute this information to them. However, I can say that the chapter on ethics at work is attributed to a piece by Cherrington and Cherrington's (1992) typology of ethical lapses in business titled 'A Menu of Moral Issues: One Week in the Life of The Wall Street Journal'.

If you are inclined to learn more on this topic, I'd recommend looking further into this piece of writing. It certainly helped me identify workplace behaviours objectively and put them into context. It also helped give me confidence in my own opinion. If you wrote that paper and would like to be credited, please do get in touch!

All too often, when you see or experience something a bit off at work, it's hard to know if you are overreacting, since it was something small or innocuous. In this scenario, listening to your instincts is the best way to gauge things. If your instincts tell you things are a bit off, they probably are. However, knowing just a little about ethics will help you assess any dilemmas you might run into at any time in the process of stabilising the team.

Applied business ethics has evolved over the centuries to ensure companies adhere to ethical standards in trade and do not fall foul of deceitful practices or opportunistic behaviours, such as:

- bribery
- nepotism in key positions

- vendor bullying
- strategic alliances that create duopolies in regulated markets
- community damage, such as illegally dumping waste or using unqualified personnel at cheap rates in a regulated industry

So what about the employees and *their* behaviour? Is there anything to be learned from internal ethics that can help take a team from storming to norming and beyond?

Absolutely there is.

In their review of over 60 articles on ethics from the *Wall Street Journal*, J. Owen Cherrington and David J. Cherrington discovered that there are 12 prominent issues affecting individuals at work. They shouldn't be surprising, but let's go through them briefly.

Stealing: It might seem okay to take a pen or two from work, but it's stealing nonetheless. If it was one pen, then the impact probably isn't going to send the company under. But what if 50 or 100 people start stealing pens, and not just one or two, but a whole box? That's quite different. And of course, stealing doesn't just include physical things. Unethical behaviour can also see people pretending to be at work while working from home, but actually be working for a second client at the same time. Or not working at all and still logging it as a paid workday.

Lying: It is not uncommon for people to stretch the truth in order to get a job, keep a job or gain a promotion.

It's human nature to lie under these circumstances, especially when working in a toxic environment underpinned by a sink-or-swim ethos. As demonstrated at the beginning of this chapter, lying comes in all shapes and sizes. Even an omission is a form of lying. Lying is closely related to fraud and deceit.

'Everyone lies.' - House

Fraud and deceit: This occurs when you allow others to take the blame for your mistakes, or you take full credit for work you didn't do, or only partially did, without stating it wasn't just your input.

Bribing and other conflicts of interest: This is a hot topic for both external and internal business ethics. Accepting under-the-table gifts from a favourite employee right before an internal interview is an obvious no-no. Other internal conflicts of interest include hiring friends without interviewing or nepotism.

Knowingly hiding information: When a business hides information from its customers, in order to win a sale, it can result in obvious commercial risk if the thing that was hidden causes harm. When employees hide information from each other, as a means of setting up individuals they don't like, or perhaps to steal the limelight at the right time in front of management, this can cause both delays and team friction.

Cheating for unfair advantage: Like lying, some people will go to great lengths to secure a job or a promotion. Anything from coercing a colleague into providing interview questions beforehand, to stealing work ideas and presenting them in a private meeting to someone of influence, are good examples of unethical internal cheating. And what about the employee who has a close relationship with the CEO and uses that to get what they want, even if it is contrary to your team's plan?

Personal decadence: I love this one! We laugh about things like this at work, because we simply put it down to 'that quirky guy who naps in the toilet'. But personal decadence can be very destructive to a team's outcomes. Here are a few examples:

- Intentionally working slowly, rather than adjusting to the team's pace
- Taking drugs or drinking alcohol at work
- Secretly sleeping on the job for hours

With each of these, it is easy to see how some things are clearly a breach of ethics at work. Drinking on the job that isn't approved, or secretly working for another company whilst billing a current employer, are clearly not ethical things to do. Stealing a PC from the office is also not great. But what about taking a pen? Or taking a 15-minute power nap in the toilet if you are a parent and have small children to tend to throughout the night? Would you consider these actions so unethical that they require attention from HR?

I believe that understanding ethics will make you, not only a better team leader, but will help make you a better human, able to successfully navigate this complicated thing call life. Understanding ethics, along with morale philosophy, will give you a foundation to work with, but be aware that it is not a black-and-white landscape. Nothing exists in a vacuum, and as you identify dilemmas and problems at work, you will soon come to see there are no clear rules, and the analysis you undertake to figure out what's going on, will oftentimes be vague at best. On each side of the dilemma will be arguments for and against that will be seemingly justifiable.

How do you learn to deal with it when there is so much grey?

For my money, a strong team charter, with an agreed set of values, is a good start. And to complement that, knowing yourself as a person, and your own ethical boundaries, will give you a good framework to start with.

For example, when building my teams, I put trust, respect and team morale at the top of the list. I don't care how fabulous one individual might be at the technicalities of their job. If they behave in a manner that causes the rest of the team to switch off and disengage, they are not a good team member, and I will usually look to find them opportunities elsewhere. Bullying, undermining, stealing ideas, exclusion and lying are behaviours you will come across in your career as a team leader. How you deal with it (or not) is up to you.

Exercise Time:

Here are some examples that I've experienced over the years. To see how effective you are at recognising potential unethical behaviours, try to rate them based on what you've just learnt.

A team's junior member is ignored for several years, regardless of efforts to assimilate. One senior brushes him off as being 'not up to my standards'.

During a meeting, while giving a status update on a late-running project you recently inherited, a director secretly texts one of the developers, who says *his* work will take two weeks. The manager openly challenges you, stating that he has just texted so-and-so, who said he would take two weeks, after you have said eight weeks. The developer is merely one small part of the chain.

You attend a meeting, during which an application architect suggests your plans are incorrect, then proceeds to use humiliating language and point out all the errors in your dependencies. You reviewed the project with the architect before the meeting to ensure it was achievable and correct. The application architect then approaches you after the meeting, gloating about his victory, and freely admits that he was testing to see if you were up to the job. He didn't hire you and was your peer, not your boss.

A recently promoted colleague says he has provided a thorough and exemplary handover to his new replacement, who is publicly struggling. The new replacement says that is not the case, and upon asking the promoted colleague about this, he starts to bark that his replacement is incompetent, so why would he bother wasting his time.

A team member seems to take forever to explain things, without getting to the point. It takes four times as long as it should, and after being asked to provide the information without the background information directly, he refuses to do so. You feel he is stalling and likes the world to revolve around him. Others think the same, and it is holding up project progress.

A new subject matter expert joins your team, except she isn't an expert. A recent hire to the company, she has no experience of complex accounting procedures, and she was provided so you could train her in the business procedures. You realise, after some time, that the business stakeholders are too busy to teach her

on the subject matter and expect you to do it.
It is entirely outside your scope as a system
test manager, and the project suffers as a result,
since she cannot verify test results. The unfortu-
nate young girl suffers stress as a result.

The fact of the matter is, all of these examples above
pose ethical dilemmas. Notwithstanding the fact that some
of them are downright manipulative and inexcusably rude,
they cross the line and can cause major friction in a team.

In isolation, these things might seem inconsequen-
tial, but repeated over periods of months or years they can
cause friction and damage in the team in a way that may
be irreparable. Friction that arises from unethical actions
can cause a person to feel all sorts of emotion, depending
on their background, culture or experience. And if the line
is badly crossed, team morale will be compromised, if not
immediately, most definitely at some point in the future.

As you've probably figured out by now, becoming
familiar with identifying unethical behaviour at work
helps you to assess how deep into the storming phase they
are. Apologies for the darkness here, but some people will
stoop to all kinds of lows, where careers, promotions, ideas
and personal advancement are concerned. But they may
not even know they are doing it. Such is the toxic culture
that swims through large, long-standing corporations. I
personally find the behaviours and reactions of individuals

from these environments rather startling. Even after two decades, people still shock the biscuits outta me!

If you are still not confident of your observational powers, then I encourage you to do two things:

1. Listen to your gut instincts. They are activated for a reason and should *never* be ignored.
2. Journal what happened, and reflectively analyse the situation to ensure you are being objective. Keep in mind, you are not trying to find the underlying causes of the unethical action, just recording that it happened.

Getting to the bottom of the cause of low team morale and dealing with unethical behaviour can be a shady business. Mostly, you may feel less like a team leader and more like a therapist. I'm afraid it comes with the territory. Not only do you have to keep your eye on the work they are doing and the processes they do (or don't) follow to assure the quality of their outputs, but you also have to turn your *people* radar on the minute you start your day so as to pick any weird or destructive behaviours.

An intelligent team leader understands the importance of team morale and seeks to create an environment where people feel good about themselves and feel connected to the work. Once people feel connected to the work, in a safe, trusted environment, you will start to experience the thing that all businesses strive for in their operations: momentum.

As a leader dealing with a messy team, you will have a lot of objectives and goals, but momentum should be at the top of the list.

Momentum is the strength gained by the forward motion of a series of events. Nothing depletes a person's reserves at work more than the lack of progress and momentum. Why? Because, let's be honest here, work isn't always rainbows and fairy dust.

Unfortunately, no matter how much you love your job, it isn't always going to be a fabulous west-end production. Insert jazz-hands. Work is hard, never-ending, and for a lot of the time, it can even be quite dull. You need a certain amount of grit to get through the day, weeks and months, and so focussing on momentum is essential. People will accept all kinds of *glum* at work, as long as they experience *progress,* combined with a pleasant and agreeable workplace. It's for this reason, everything you do along the way to move a team from storming phase to performing, should be done using the idea of momentum.

Foster connection, build trust, create safety, increase morale, and produce momentum. Et voilà! Productive team.

Oh, how complicated this handful of words is. It has taken me a good couple of decades to amass the experience to figure out how to fix messy teams using the theory of momentum. And truth be told, I'm still learning! Without a doubt, it works, but it is hard work. And so my aim in this series of instructional handbooks is to teach you all that

I've learnt, so you can cut to the chase quickly and avoid the painful mistakes I've made.

SECTION 2

Stabilising the Team

You've heard of the saying 'learn to walk before you run'? In this context, it's 'stabilise before you accelerate'. I know, it's not exactly catchy or mind-blowing, but it's essentially what you will be working towards.

Before you can get a team to increase their output and accelerate their velocity, you will need to go through a period of stabilisation. The purpose of stabilisation is to calm the storm, giving you an opportunity to surface the underlying issues and get to the root cause of them.

A storming team needs to come back to basics, and during this time, you need to focus on making things simple. This is a tough call in technology, as we have a tendency to over-complicate things, and I think this is a big part of why teams run amok. Complexity feels good to the analytical mind. There is a sense of pride when the analytical mind stumbles across complex problems and solves them with complicated solutions. But if a team is left to their own devices, it is for sure they will go down the rabbit hole, making it difficult and painful for any team leader to extract them.

Warning: Stabilising your team will feel uncomfortable, because the techniques you follow may look elementary. The more technical your team is, the more uncomfortable they will feel. Be prepared for some backlash during this stage. No matter how basic they may feel it is, this process works. Just keep your focus on the end goal, and take any negative or passive-aggressive comments that may come your way with a grain of salt. The bottom line is, if there were already one individual member in the team smart enough to figure out how to get them into the productive performing stage, you wouldn't be there.

CHAPTER 6

Where Am I?

By this stage, I hope I've armed you with enough information to spark your interest and motivate you to want it. I'm always excited at the prospect of fixing a messy team. In general conversations with colleagues and peers outside of my day job, I light up the minute someone complains about an unproductive team or disruptive team member. If this happens to you, you're on the right track, and most likely ready to dive in, which is tempting. But before you do, take a step back and relax.

It's never a good idea to dive in head first to something like this, as you risk your enthusiasm for success taking precedence and blocking your ability to see what's going on. A mistake I've personally made many times. Your first step in this process is to understand more about your team as a group by using the principles you learnt in the previous chapter on Tuckman's Group Development model. Never believe what you see at first sight. The problems you see immediately tend to be manifestations of deeper issues.

Are they storming, and if so, how bad is it? Or are they still in the forming stage, because people keep leaving every few weeks, and they have to spend time getting used to a new team member? Maybe they're performing, but only when given a specific area of the application to work on, indicating a skills shortage.

Lots of questions! First, let's start by:

1. Observing the team and making some notes. Request to be invited to all calls and meetings that are coming up, be they one-offs or recurring. The more time you can spend observing what they are doing, the better.

2. Noting the culture during their meetings and interactions. Do they have a set of objectives? Can meetings be tied back to a group of tasks in the plan? Are they open, and does everyone communicate freely, or do they participate in closed, quippy dialogue? What about their mission? Is what they are doing tied back to something measurable? Culture is difficult to pin down at first, but continued observation and analysis of what you witness will help ascertain the root causes.

3. Keeping a journal and completing the templates in the back of this book for group development and communication styles. As you journal your observations, try dividing your learnings into three categories: people, politics or process. Or all three. You

are not looking for a root cause, just a sense of how they work to get the job done.

The length of your observation period will depend entirely on the size and complexity of the team, company and technology stack. As a rule of thumb, you probably want to do nothing but observe and blend into the current process for at least the first two to four weeks. If you steam ahead like a bull at a gate too quickly, you risk misunderstanding nuances that could see your work come undone months or years into the process. Nuances that might have you rethink things very early to avoid wasting time and money. The point is, before you run at that gate, don't assume it's locked. It might look locked, but it may turn out to be only partially latched, and you could end up falling through it and straight on your face.

A premature diagnosis of a team's real problems is not a good thing, because usually, the first problem you address is not the *only* problem. And fixing that single problem will not result in a magical unicorn team.

Dysfunctional teams tend to reveal themselves like onion layers. Like the Greek goddess Medusa, cutting off one snake will see another appear in its place, ready to strike, and sometimes you won't see it coming.

Observe, observe, observe.

You will need to watch and listen carefully, not only when they interact, but also when they *don't* interact.

How do they communicate with each other? Do they all tend towards the same style, or does one-half of the team get to the point quickly, while one or two others like to meander around the houses, and the rest lose interest?

Do they pay lip service and use counterfeit commitments to get off calls or out of the room?

Is there passive-aggressive sarcasm or outright rudeness?

Do they seem supportive of one another, or do they continually push 'my way is the best way'?

Getting to grips with how people work as a group and their underlying motives as individuals is the key to your success.

'We see people not as they are but as they appear to us. And these appearances are usually misleading.' Robert Greene, *The Laws of Human Nature*

The most essential skill you need as a team leader is an ability to observe without judgement or bias and interpret those observations into problem statements.

When you're working with a storming team, everything you do – process improvement, team changes, even your own personal leadership improvement – serves one purpose, transformation. And transformation is a process of change, which at any time can go in one of two directions, good or bad. Understanding whether you are headed in the right direction or not comes down to astute observation and analysis of where you are today.

The sooner you learn to identify where your team is and what actions you need to take, the sooner you will be able to influence the change needed for success.

So many people spend time formulating a vision for what they want the team to look like. And I do suggest you define your end goal, but before you can take the journey to a destination, you need a starting point. If my friend and I both want to fly to New York, but they are in Los Angeles, and I am in London, it would be foolish to think each of our trips would be the same, because we are starting from different places. It seems obvious when you put it like that, but surprisingly, at work, not many people stop and take stock of where they currently are before embarking on improvements. We are living in a results-driven culture that makes us focus on end goals. But ignoring the 'where am I?' question may send you off in a direction that may not necessarily be right.

When you start observing your team in action, you are looking for clues that indicate where they are.

Once you have enough information about the people and the processes they use, it's time to document this and figure out where they are. This is an example of a simple template that I like to use. If you have no system of your own to collate observations and diagnose team issues, then feel free to use the example templates in this book.

How often you use this template is dependent on your team, and the problems within. I have created this template to help you address two types of messy team situations. They are;

- Acute: these are teams that show signs of mild friction caused by everyday issues that arise in teams from time to time. For this situation, you should use all sections of the template.
- Chronic: these are ongoing, longer term problems that destructively impact a team's ability to function. For these situations, you will probably use the top two sections across a series of forms before drafting a problem statement.

As you being your observation, you may find the need to use more than one template, this is typical for chronic situations. Use your intuition to tell you what is the right amount, but as a rule of thumb, I like to use;

- One for the major meetings that exceed an hour.
- One for each day to summarise findings
- Then one at the end of the week which pulls together the main points in order to establish patterns.

What did you see?	Explain the context?
Write down what you saw, what was said, what actions were taken. Be objective and stick to plain facts	Was it a meeting, any extenuating circumstances, who else was involved at the time or behind the scenes? Has this happened before? Is it a one off or a trend in the team?

Decision time	Viable actions to take.
What can you do to address it short term/long term? Is this something you can resolve or do you need outside help?	If you can address the issue, write the steps down you will take, in order to resolve or start to help with the issue.

I have used templates like these over the years and I evolve and change them with every team I take on, so I encourage you to do the same for your journey.

Once you have this information gathered, the next step is to establish a picture of what the team needs to look like, or the end game? Read the next chapter to establish how to determine your teams end game.

CHAPTER 7

The End Game

This is where things start to get creative. You now have to decide what the end game is going to look like. Or what you and your client/stakeholders want it to look like. When you create this 'to-be vision', there are a few things that you are going to need to consider.

> Defining a textbook-perfect end vision will inevitably lead to disaster. Your team is unique, and it is vital to consider the individuals' uniqueness and the circumstances surrounding them as a team. I once had to spend nearly seven months trying to coach a project manager who could not write, let alone communicate, a project plan to his team. It was painful, but in addition to that, the person suffered from anxiety and could not deal with conflict. No amount of process work on my part was ever going to resolve the issues, as he wasn't a fit

for the job. He hated the position, was deeply demotivated and came to the table every day demonstrating little to no applied learning. Regardless of what others might tell you about being a great leader, these sorts of personnel issues are pretty commonplace, and they can be very detrimental when trying to transform a team. If you have severe people issues inside a storming team, your strategy is not worth the paper it's written on. I recommend creating a vision for what the team should look like in two years and track your progress toward that.

You may need help defining an end game. Lots of transformation specialists will tell you it's imperative to lay down grand plans for the future. They are usually consultants and are commercially obliged to show what they are doing for their fees. If your leadership team has been dealing with a frustrated, living hell of a non-performing team, then they may see you as the messiah, and not giving them the promised land will weaken their confidence in you. But suppose your observation period results in findings that heavily revolve around gaps in skillsets or unethical behaviours. In that case, you will have to deal with those first, so writing a plan will be almost impossible. You can strategise what you will do, but rarely can you plan it, because people react how they want to, not how your *plan* wants them to.

Where management is concerned, you will gain more of their trust and confidence by openly stating the difficulties in predicting the future where there is so much instability. Instead, it would help if you created quarterly short-term goals that will pivot according to the outcomes achieved.

Some people refer to it as politics. I call it dramatic theatre. To avoid getting embroiled in people's opinions, you always have to guard your 'Spidy Sense'. People will try to pull you in all directions to suit their purpose. To avoid misinterpreting information, you should focus on the roles people are required to fill and the skill level required to deliver the work. You may need to rebuild this team's structure, so noting missing skill sets early on will be helpful. Unfortunately, you can't separate the person from how they use their skills to deliver the work. It is very tricky trying to fix a team when there are members behaving in a way that sabotages progress. So be mindful as you go through this period, that observation is a learnt skill, and can be a difficult one to master, because humans are flawed creatures in the way we think, which means we all bring bias to the table, no matter what.

Bow what?

Once you have the picture of where you are and where you want to be, it's time to consider building a roadmap. Your roadmap will consist of a problem statement and a series of quick wins designed to stabilise the team and sort out any negative feelings. If you are specifically dealing with a chronically messy team it's your job to figure out each problem area, then prescribe a short term fix that will move the team towards the norming phase as quickly as possible. Simple, right?

Well…

If transformation were that easy, then you wouldn't be reading this book, and there would be no need for my 'fix-it' services.

So where do you start?

This is where you will take your observational data and try to succinctly explain the problems you have seen. I'd recommend you draft your observations to begin with, and try to sort them into a cohesive picture. When you start drafting, you will need to be your own observer, to make sure you don't draft *opinions*. Opinions are the crux of your own bias, and so can sometimes provide distorted reality.

A quick example of a bad and good problem statement looks like this:

> Bad: The senior team members have an air of superiority about them, causing them to ignore or dismiss the juniors during discussion.

> Good: During discussion, and when attempting to participate, the junior team members are either talked over or their comments are quickly dismissed. Statements such as 'you don't know the system well enough to say that' have been heard.

The first one is your perspective (that the senior team members feel superior), which may or may not be correct. Simply put, it is just your opinion. Down the line, other evidence may come to the surface that confirms this as being true, but you are far better placed to just explain what you see and hear at this point of the journey, *factually*, in order to better understand the true issues.

The first problem statement might lead you to believe the only solution is to get rid of the arrogant so-and-so, since he is clearly causing problems within the team.

But using the second statement as your basis, should make you think 'Hang on, the juniors don't know the system?'

Apart from the fact that they are juniors, surely, they know something of the system. Why don't they know the system? Because they get no training.

> Why don't they get training? Because there isn't time for training.

> Why isn't there time for training? Because the management set milestones without proper

estimating, and the team are constantly in 'hurry up' mode. Tempers are frayed, time is short and no one feels comfortable saying so.

Why don't management allow for proper estimating? That's a whole other Pandora's box!

See what I mean? You could potentially do the same analysis on the first statement, and go down a very different path, to a very different outcome.

Why do they act that way and be rude? Because they are unhappy (opinion).

Why are they unhappy? Insert a million different reasons.

Dead end.

In my humble experience, when we use unbiased statements to record the problems, it releases our train of thought from personal opinions and views, and allows us to think analytically about *what* is happening, not what we *perceive to be* happening.

You know the way your brain has a habit of producing thoughts based on what or how you are focussing on something at the time? For example, if you are thinking angry thoughts, it tends to perpetuate more angry thoughts, and if you're not careful, you could end up in a vicious cycle and spiral down to a place you shouldn't be. Guard your thoughts, keep them neutral and focus on facts. You'll be far more successful in the long run.

So now it's your turn.

Take a look at this example below.

Problem Statement: Based on three weeks of full-time, on-site observation, the following behaviours have been identified:

Process

Several members of the team do not actively participate in meetings. Only four individuals out of ten speak regularly, and the rest listen. The meetings arc more or less a conversation between these four people, which the team are observing.

Meetings constantly run over time, and there is no meeting purpose or goal set. The conversations seem to address minute issues that are going on in the moment.

There are no meetings to discuss strategy, approach or planning.

The team produce no documentation throughout the project life cycle, with the exception of schematic diagrams at the beginning, which they create on a whiteboard but never transfer to soft copy. Two members of the team work in different locations, making it difficult. The response to this is taking a photo of the diagram and emailing it. The schematic design is rarely updated.

They don't log defects. They use email or chat to communicate defects in the software and simply fix on the spot before shipping to test. There is no information for the test team about whether the software behaviour has changed as a result of incorrect design, and no root cause analysis is performed. At this stage, it looks like they might be repeating design flaws.

People

As per the meeting, there seems to be an 'old lion' effect going on in this team. Four individuals hold the knowledge, and no training is provided to the junior members. The four 'old lions' hold the floor in all discussions, and the other team members are not given valid explanations as to why a decision is being made or how the software evolved to this point.

The juniors are dismissed by the seniors in meetings and are allocated minimal work.

Team leaders are directive and use a 'just do it' approach to meeting milestones. 80% of the team are apathetic to their jobs, but this will need to be uncovered in interviews.

Thinking of the observations you have made of your team, and using the example problem statement above as a guide, try to write your own problem statements.

To help, there is a template in the back of the book titled 'Problem Statement'. Fill in the first column with the problem paragraph, then complete the second column with a quick recommendation.

Problem Statement	Process
	Write your thoughts on the process they follow to get their work done. You will need to note things they do well, things that need refining or things they don't do at all.

People

Make any notes about how the team interact with each other, and the general sentiment and atmosphere. Use the Guides in the back of the book which outline the four stages of Tuckman's Group Development.

Conclusion

This is where you will write up your conclusion on the state of the team, the current problems as you view them.

Now that you have an idea of the first-level problems (there will be more), you can go through them and decide what actions you need to take to rectify.

Once you have done that and are happy, go through and find three things you believe will make a big difference in the short term and that you think you have a good chance of implementing and seeing results on inside three to four months. These are called your 'quick wins'. We will talk more about quick wins in the next chapter.

CHAPTER 8

Quick Wins

Although I'm not an advocate for getting stuck into, well, anything, without a bit of thought and planning, your manager is probably going to want to see action and ROI for your being there pretty fast. To be successful in this space of cleaning up messy teams, you should think about quick wins straight off the bat. This will help in a couple of ways:

1. It will establish your position in the team early on and give you a chance to learn the culture and political aspects of the group.
2. It will give your client or management a sense of confidence that you know what you are doing and that they hired right.

Quick wins create momentum by leveraging something called 'recency bias'. All you have to do is facilitate a few new changes that are aimed at stabilising the weak points from your observation period and recency bias will naturally encourage the individuals to continue with more change. What is recency bias?

Have you ever finished a bad relationship, then found yourself avoiding dating because 'all relationships suck'? Whenever you go through a bad experience, your emotional disturbance leads you to make conclusions that drive decision-making based on that recent event.

I read somewhere recently that the brain can't make decisions without emotion, and if this is true, it certainly puts recency bias into context. You may have noticed it yourself, that following highly charged emotional events, your perspective changes and questionable decisions follow suit.

The same can be said of a positive situation. If you have a fantastic family holiday, you oftentimes want to repeat it. Get amazing service at a shop you've never liked before, and it will change your opinion, and you will go back again.

Recency bias is a behavioural bias that says that our most recent experiences, be they good or bad, impact decision-making. When a team has been experiencing all the negative and unproductive patterns of the storming phase, it is difficult for them to be truly objective, to move forward. The immediacy of recent events, especially if they were over a long period of time, will impair their ability to trust in their own decisions. Human memory and intuition, although very powerful tools for our survival, can turn against us if we don't know what to look out for.

Quick wins allow you to leverage *positive* recency bias by putting distance between the good outcomes of today, and the bad experiences from yesterday. If you don't get some wins immediately and try to implement a long, drawn-out process in the far-off distance, you risk the team always sitting with the last negative, unproductive memories of work.

It is difficult for a team to trust a newcomer, and it is even more difficult for them to think about long-term, perfect-process goals with so much friction. Keep in mind, some of them, or maybe all of them, will be exhausted from the drama and wary of anyone claiming to have the tools to fix it all.

If you do it right, a series of quick wins will get the team working more cohesively and should start to change the atmosphere enough for them to see that positive change is possible.

When choosing your quick wins, keep in mind what you are trying to achieve in relation to group development.

I'd recommend choosing no more than three, maybe four, if you think the team can handle it. Change is painful for some people. Although we tend to avoid emotional terms like that in the office environment, it's true. So select some low-hanging fruit that doesn't require a lot of effort, budget or authorisation to implement. Something local. Here are a few ideas:

> The first powerful quick win for a storming team is the 'team charter'. If they have a team

charter, perhaps it's time to revisit it. A good idea is to include a team working agreement. If they don't have one, then this should be your very first step.

Include a purpose and goal on every meeting invitation. And take minutes or record the meeting if it is online.

Implement core coding/working hours in the day to allow for an increase in productivity. Unless they are so insular that communication has broken down, in which case you may need to go the opposite direction, by creating collaborative sessions for work items instead.

Only have key individuals in meetings. Three or four people is the maximum for efficiency.

Ask them to rough draft a design with a few rules and acceptance criteria before they start coding and present it to the team.

Think about the review process of documents and artefacts.

If there is a shortfall in the team with knowledge, introduce a 'buddy up'.

Think about exposing more information with regular reporting on progress. Both inside the team and outside.

Set goals. Every time they have to produce something, set the goal. What is the end game, and why are they doing it? What should their deliverable look like? Get specific with them or they will produce something very different.

Quick wins are essential, and you should not overlook this part of your journey. In fact, if this is an ongoing team leadership role, you may find the need to do quick wins from time to time to improve constantly changing situations. What you're aiming for with quick wins is the introduction of clarity, to give your team a sense of control and purpose.

'Stress can be attributed to uncertainty, lack of information and sensing a loss of control.'
Gabor Maté

Note: The key to successful quick wins is choosing things that are within their reach and that you have the power to implement locally without going through layers of approval. A bad example of a quick win would be to try and introduce a training discipline, because it will take weeks, if not months, of negotiation for the budget, before you even get to consider hiring training professionals. Not to mention the logistics of finding them desk space, integrating them into the team, etc. You get the point.

Choose things that you can do inside the team, without budget, and that they can immediately implement.

Over the first 10 to 12 weeks, these small, quick wins, if repeated regularly and with discipline, will build confidence and create momentum. If you have an untethered team that is all over the place from one day to the next, even adding in a daily stand-up meeting will help. I believe the 15-minute morning meeting is the most underestimated in terms of impact and intel. I have uncovered some pretty shady goings-on through the simple daily stand-up meeting, ranging from developers who have more than four hours capacity a day, to principal developers who believe they are above reporting their progress.

The objective in these first few weeks or months, is not to implement perfect-process or instantly improve productivity. If your team has been in storming for a long time, you have to fix the relationships between the people first.

This is, unfortunately, something few team leaders want to address, and even fewer management understand. There is a tendency in this space to go about fixing the process first, by implementing complex project plans, alongside over-the-top progress reports, using PowerPoint. But that would be a mistake. Even if you managed to produce a perfect project plan with aligned dependencies and resources correctly assigned, it requires a healthy, positive and motivated set of individuals to execute the tasks in the plan. How do you suppose they will do that, if they are demotivated, low in energy and exhibit little trust between them?

The French have a saying, *mettre en valeur*. It means to prioritise, or to focus on. If you have a team that is in the forming phase and just needs a bit of organising, then focussing on implementing process is ideal.

The 'process-driven' approach may work if your team is in forming, and there are no major issues impeding progress. But if your team has been in storming, and it's been going on for months, or even years, you will have no choice but to bring together a group of individuals who are at war and encourage them to positively interact with each other to create a more engaging atmosphere.

Quick wins are designed to give your team confidence and blow a bit of fresh air into a stagnant atmosphere. Using the outcomes from the Problem Statement template completed in the previous chapter, decide what activities and tasks could be used as quick wins.

Remember to:

1. Choose things that you can implement yourself locally and without approval.

2. Coach your team along the way so they know what's coming. They are not required to know the entire details, since you may have to figure that out as you go along. But some coaching and reassurance will be beneficial.

3. Decide on the quick wins yourself. In the initial stages of the transformation, avoid asking for their opinions on whether the quick win is appropriate

or not. When the team is in the storming phase, emotions will most likely be running high, and bias will play a big part in their decision-making. You are most likely the only objective party, approaching the team from a bird's-eye view, so only you can really determine what is best in terms of their transformation towards norming.

4. Observe, reflect, and pivot as needed. Give your quick wins some time to bed in, but keep your eye on anything that doesn't seem to be working and adapt quickly.

5. Take baby steps to avoid confusion and resistance. Try not to take on any more than two or three changes every couple of months. Transformation takes a long time, and it tends to move at their pace, not yours.

SECTION 3

Next Steps

As the first few weeks pass, the complexities will likely start to unravel, and you will see how layered your team is. Not only in terms of the work itself but also the people.

More likely than not, you will uncover a number of ah-ha moments that will make you question your powers of observation and assessment. This is a good thing. No one is an expert in this stuff, and if you find these ah-ha moments, you are now learning.

The person you thought was upsetting the apple cart at the beginning of your journey may simply be reacting to the well-hidden machinations of another team member that weren't apparent to you. Or perhaps the fact that half the team lacks the basic skills to get their job done is less to do with the lack of training and more with a non-existent recruitment policy.

As you progress deeper into your transformation, things may start to look different, and you will be required to go back to your observations and start again in some places. Remember in Chapter 7, where we discussed the need for mindful observation and to regard events and facts over jumping to conclusions based on judgement?

It's challenging for humans to avoid making judgements, and as things unfold, you'll soon start to see your patterns of bias. Learn from them and look at how you need to adapt and pivot your approach to keep your team on the straight and narrow.

CHAPTER 9

Going Beyond Quick Wins

Well done! You have managed to make it past the first step towards stabilising your team. Once you have established a few quick wins, and after at least three to six months, you will need to start thinking about really shifting the team to a different model of delivery.

This is where two things are probably going to happen:

The team may *de-stabilise* as you introduce greater change that is outside their comfort zone, so it's a good idea to discuss this with your stakeholders up front, so they are aware of what is to come. It's also a good idea to discuss it with the team, and often.

Your acceleration will stall because of the politics and games people start to play as you implement change they don't agree with. As a result, both the team and management may become disheartened, and begin to voice their doubts about your progress and whether the situation really is fixable. After weeks or months of seeing you 'hit it outta the park' with a handful of quick wins, energy and enthusiasm will abound with the work you're doing. Problem is, a lot of people don't understand transformation, and so think your trajectory for success is going to be linear and continual. Naturally, when you hit a speed bump, things will slow a bit, before they take off again.

There isn't an instant solution to team problems. Be aware that they will probably crop up, and the team will move in and out of group phases as you get into the depths of it. It takes time to fix messy teams, and these days, few companies are willing to make the investment. Over the decades, I've noticed companies outsourcing their delivery teams to offshore suppliers, thinking it will solve the issues. Sometimes it does, but sometimes it doesn't.

It once took me a year to figure out the root cause of some serious issues in a storming team, which had been deemed to be the fault of one individual in the team. The person was considered to be the 'demon child' of developers, who did what he wanted, when he wanted, pumping out random functionality at random intervals. But upon further inspection and the passage of time, he was, in fact, the product of a bigger and more serious problem.

There was no clear strategy in place, so he was never provided with any clear direction from the leadership team. As a result, he had evolved into someone who got on with doing what he believed to be correct. Unfortunately, it turned out, what he believed to be important wasn't strictly correct, but without clear direction and priorities, how was it his fault?

Of course, by the time the issue was addressed, he had become used to being in charge of, well, everything and struggled to transition, causing the team to go deeper into the storming phase.

The point I'm trying to make is that, once you start implementing your quick wins, things will surface that you never realised were even there. So it's important to continue observing your team and assessing what needs doing as you go along.

This is where I probably differ from other transformation specialists in that I believe you should take your lead from the team dynamics, rather than force them into a place they don't belong. Why? Because the alternative is firing the so-called troublemakers and recruiting in the perfect employee, who slots into the team in a happy and harmonious manner. If you've been through recruitment before, you'll know the perfect employee doesn't exist.

Beyond the quick wins is when you should start looking at the operations inside your team and the delivery framework or model, with a view to implementing processes bit by bit, so that you have a cohesive delivery methodology.

You may continue implementing quick wins now and again, and I encourage that, as it's quite effective. But after the first few months of this, it's time to move into the depths of your team and tackle the bigger issues.

This is where your subject matter comes into play, and you need to determine with the team and your line management, what improvements come next. Getting the team stabilised and into the norming phase, is a feat in and of itself, so now is a good time to let the team just be for a while.

Constant change is exhausting, especially for team leaders. Take a breath, regroup and go back to your observation phase to see which direction to take.

CHAPTER 10

24 Things I Know About the Art of Leadership (Although I'm Sure There Are Probably More)

In closing, I'd like to introduce you to few key concepts that I believe are worth their weight in gold. These are things you'll want to consider, some of them philosophical, that will help in your daily life to become a more intelligent team leader.

The topic of intelligent leadership is one that could fill an entire volume of encyclopaedias, but I'm going to give you a few ideas that you can ponder, to see if anything sparks your interest enough to dig further into your own research and learnings. Leadership is a lifetime skill.

1. As a manager, you've probably been taught to do things that you can prove in advance – that's planning. Planning is a 'to-do list' and is often difficult

to pull off in technology environments, because project outcomes are usually different. The waterfall method spawned from the manufacturing industry, where widgets come off a production line, and tasks are identical from one part to the next. This is where planning works – in a highly controlled, highly predictable environment. But product companies who produce things that are iterations or improvements on a base offering, or who are trying to innovate their product portfolio, do not create identical outcomes. This hidden element of planning and technology delivery usually underpins failed delivery, resulting in unhappy, demotivated teams.

2. *Strategy* is based on a hypothesis and requires acceptance that things will go wrong. Laying down logic, based on assumptions, will give you the power to pivot when your assumptions change, or new constraints come to light. To create a strategy, you need to decide the outcomes you want in the future and then decide what guiding actions you should take. Objectives, not prescribed processes, deliver *strategy*. Although some process needs to happen in the trenches, your transformation should be intuitive and responsive to the team.

3. *Planning* is based on known things and specific target outputs. *Strategy* will mostly contain assumptions and views of 'what needs to be true for this to

happen'. Managers use planning to get things done; leaders use strategy.

4. Estimating is, by and large, impossible to do with any certainty, unless you are producing the exact same thing, using the exact same tools, run by the same people – every time.

5. Most people prefer plans, because they seemingly 'predict the future', providing a sense of control, and control means comfort. Have you ever heard of a predictable future? I haven't. There are future states you can predict with certainty. If you eat a pack of six donuts every day for a month, it's highly likely you'll gain weight and develop health issues. But the world of technology delivery is more complicated, and if your company is in a highly competitive, highly volatile market, the future is impossible to predict with any sense of certainty.

6. Some days are going to be fabulous, and other days are going to suck. That's just life in general, and especially true of life as a team leader.

7. Try to avoid fitting a square peg into a round hole to tick a problem-solving box on your list.

8. Individuals in your team don't decide if they are good enough to stay in the game. You do. If someone isn't performing, and the impact is visible in the team or team's outputs, it's time to put your player on the bench.

9. Everyone will complain because everyone has a point of view. They are rarely correct and usually come from the individual's set of biases. Unless you have hard evidence to support the complaints, take what other people tell you with a grain of salt and stay on your path. Only you truly see and understand what is going on in your team.

10. If you suck at observation, you will suck at being a team leader.

11. People do and think what they want, even within the bounds of an employment contract. If what they do and think contradicts the team's ethics, values and reason for existence, then the person needs to move on.

12. Diversity is your best weapon against mediocre results.

13. If you are closed-minded and need everything to be defined inside tight boundaries, you will never develop the mental capabilities to help find solutions for really complex problems.

14. Your team and company will live or die by their ability to recruit and retain fantastic talent. That doesn't mean you hire only superstars. You need a balance of levels across the board; otherwise, the superstars will end up fighting amongst themselves and mostly for attention. Think bell curve (google it!). Understand precisely why you are recruiting and the exact skills you need.

15. Your team's skills need to be valid against your delivery plans, not just for the immediate future, but for what you have to get done next year. If management is asking you to deliver changes requiring an AI skillset and you only have a team of C# front-end developers, you need to recruit quickly.

16. Not every company is led by a 'Steve Jobs'. In fact, there was only one.

17. *The 48 Laws of Power*, as written by Robert Greene, will be the best book you ever read on how to survive the perils of life inside a big company. His books *The Laws of Human Nature* and *The 33 Strategies of War* are also indispensable. In fact, learn everything you can from Robert Greene. He is really smart.

18. Sometimes, you are dealt the cards you are dealt. It may seem unappetising for you and the team to work with someone who goes against the grain, but if your recruitment budget totals zero, and the individual in question is the only person who knows your product, then you need to think of other ways to skin the cat.

19. And there is always more than one way to skin a cat. Think carefully about the pros and cons of something before making your move. Things are rarely black and white in this world. Intelligent team leaders know that.

20. Attempt to create superior virtuous cycles.

21. Use your intuition. Ignore it at your peril, but likewise, beware of recency bias. When your intuition triggers, ask yourself if this could be because of recent events that have left you feeling deflated and have tarnished your opinion. If in doubt, ask a trusted colleague close to the situation.

22. Force nothing. 無為Wu Wei, translated, means the principle of not forcing anything that you do. Allow people to hold their space in the team. If they can't, don't force it; help them move on. Implement process, but if people don't take to it and the results are mediocre, don't force it. Take action and be assertive, but only make your move at the right moment. Everything in its own time.

23. Every team leader has a reason and a season. There are peace-time leaders and war-time leaders. If you are a peace-time leader, running a great performing team in a business-as-usual mode will suit you well. If you are a war-time leader, you thrive on fixing the messiness and chaos, and so you will probably get bored once that's gone.

24. Your job as a specialist fix-it team leader is more or less done when your team leaves the storming phase and starts accelerating their outcomes. Messy teams are a specialist métier, and if you know this is your purpose and have a natural affinity to the work, it's best to start looking for your next challenge once the messiness is tidied up.

CHAPTER 11

Final Words

Messy teams are exhausting to fix but also one of the most rewarding things you will do at work. I've tried to simplify a very complex activity by giving you rinse-and-repeat-style steps that I use all the time to influence positive change in messy teams.

You'll want to understand:

1. Tuckman's Model of Group Development.
2. Ethical behaviour at work and how it affects team morale.
3. The definition of trust, what it looks like and why it is so important for performant teams.

After which you will need to:

1. Get great at observation and analysis.

2. Document where your team are, before you decide where they need to go.

3. Identify and implement some quick wins that will help stabilise the team.

4. Constantly reassess and reaffirm your observations as you go.

Like with anything, as a new team leader, it will take time, combined with repetition, to become good at fixing messy teams. The key is to start without fear. Will you get it wrong? Probably. Will it matter if you get it wrong? Yes, sometimes it will, but other times, it won't. I tend to be quite stoic about these things myself. I believe, if I mess up, it's for a reason that usually exposes itself in the future.

Team leadership is neither an just art nor a science. It's both. It takes courage, empathy, a sense of humour, honesty, humility, and grit to be good at it.

It also requires you to detach from it to succeed at it. Do your best, be conscious about your actions and decisions, but don't take any of your days to heart. Unless lives are at stake, you are not required to give every molecule of your mental health to your job. At the end of the day, you need to go home, learn to switch off, relax and get a peaceful night's sleep.

Because when tomorrow arrives, you'll need to be at your best to be an intelligent leader.

Additional Info
Welcome to OODA Loop Lane

This little section is a bit of a deviation, but I think it's important to learn some sort of method that you can use as you work with your team. Never assume that the data you collected at the beginning is going to be true in three months' time, or even true in the first place. Things will happen that will require you to reassess your position or re-evaluate the data. Get used to the idea of going through analysis on a weekly, if not daily, basis.

I like to use something called the OODA loop. I don't necessarily use it formally, and sometimes the day is so busy that I do it mentally or map it out on a scrap piece of paper so I can get to the heart of the problem and fix it. This is how it was designed to be used. Fast, and in the heat of battle.

It was created by Colonel John Boyd, quite a clever man, who served in the United States Air Force from 1945 to 1975, and he spent much of this as a military strategist holding posts in the Fighter Weapons School, then later in the Pentagon, conducting mathematical analysis for the F-15 Eagle program. He was famous for his long-standing bet, as a military strategist, that he could out defeat any pilot in manoeuvring tactics in less than 40 seconds, from a relative position of weakness.

His military theories gave way to changing the way pilots think in combat and still stand today. His relentless, but passionate, pursuit of tactical and strategical combat perfection often earned him nicknames, such as Genghis John or The Mad Major.

One of his military theories, known as the OODA loop, was developed to help pilots in combat with a systematic, unemotional approach to surviving in combat, using the observe – orient – decide – act cycle. The OODA loop. It is designed to help the user to think more rapidly, allowing them to get inside the opponent's decision-making process more quickly to gain the upper hand.

This may sound underhanded and devious to you, depending on your character, but think about how many times people tell you the real truth at work? People at work are reticent to tell the truth because they fear retribution. Nine times out of ten, they will provide you with a watered-down version of the truth, leaving out crucial information, leading you to make potential errors in your transformation work. It is imperative that you get to the root cause of the issues if you are to fix or transform them.

Today, the OODA loop is a common cycle used in continuity planning, and more recently, learning, and I encourage you to learn this theory and use it as much as you can. Without a structure to your decision-making, in the context of improving team learning and behaviours, you will most likely flounder around for longer than necessary, making decisions using potentially unhelpful information. And end up confused, bewildered at your outcomes, wondering where you went wrong.

Remember, most of the time, you are going to be working with people, and people, while wonderful, are complex and move with very unusual layers of motivation. Not all of it good.

The key to the OODA loop is that the team are not aware of the process, and so this allows you to obscure your intentions whilst getting to the heart of the real issues at hand.

The OODA loop essentially brings together cognitive science, game theory and gestalt psychology. It is predicated on the basis of ambiguity, which is to be accepted, rather than avoided. Ambiguity exists, like it or not. You are bound to come across a lot of it when you first start your transformation, and the more dysfunctional the team, the more ambiguity you are likely to find. Frustrating, right?

People will give you all sorts of misinformation and try to lead you off on a witch hunt. Don't worry, just follow these four steps every time you witness a recurring theme in your team.

> Observation – During this phase, you are looking to identify unfolding circumstances, outside information, and also the way in which that information interacts or unfolds in the team.

Orientation – Put some context around what is happening at the time and determine if the situation is justifiable and if the team are reacting to something outside them, or is it internal, or one individual, who is struggling to follow process, that is causing the upset?

Decision – From there, it will be easy to see what is going wrong and decide what you are going to do to attack it.

Action – Take action and sort the issue out. Move on.

Although the OODA loop method was primarily developed for quick-thinking situations, it can still be used for more involved situations that require careful analysis. Each time you record an event or action during the initial observation period, follow the OODA formula to be sure you are not missing out on important context.

Acknowledgment

Without a doubt, this book would not have happened if it weren't for two people.

Chandler Bolt and his unique and touching Ted talk made me realise the importance of writing and how impactful your ideas can be on the next generation. His dedication to self-publishing school is unparalleled, and his services stand head and shoulders above the rest. What a blessing to the world.

Kerk Murray is my fantastic, kind, patient and ever-present writing coach, without whom I would have thrown in the towel. I kept kicking the can down the road, but eventually, we got there. I cannot say thank you enough, and I am looking forward to lots of books and new adventures!

To every person, I have ever worked with in my career and every friend in my circle. You may not know it, but you have an enormous impact on everything I do. You challenge me, allow me to think about things differently, and force me to think of things in a way I usually don't. These interactions have enriched my professional life and flowed into my personal life, making me who I am today.

There are too many to list. Here are a few.

Mum, Dad, Simone, Megs, Claire Allen, Claire Webb, Livvy G, Gemma, Cassie, Stephen A, Aunty Wendy, Doug, Rachel Grey, Stephanie B, Martine, Sam Toye, Claire Gleeson,
Sue Roberts and Lainey!

Tuckman's Model of Group Development

Use these guides to identify where you think your team might be and get ideas on how to address the issues.

FORMING

Observations	Feelings	Needs	Your Job
• Politeness • High levels of agreeableness • Silence in meetings, or tentative interaction • Avoidance of conflict or controversy • Discussion of things not specific to the goals • Individuals may form alliances for safety	• Excitement and optimisim • Fearful or guarded • Uncertainty, why are we here? What are we doing?	• Team charter to establish working patterns between members • Goals and task that will produce a value outcome • Operational guidelines or processes to avoid assumptions on how to produce the goals • Effective team meeting culture	• Focus on optimism, and what can be done • Provide decision making and feedback fast • Actively involved in the day to day running • Re-iteration of team goals, and team charter when needed • Demonstrate confidence and focus on teamgoals

STORMING

Observations	Feelings	Needs	Your Job
• Arguments and passive sarcasm • Power plays for leadership • Misunderstanding of roles and responsiblities in practise • Individuality, and a lack of consensus • Excessive workloads for individuals • Lack of open listening and acceptance of other • Unfair judgements	• Defensiveness • Unsafe • Discomfort due to high levels of disagreement • Apathy as cycles of conflict stop progress • Questioning about things being done correctly	• Clarification of roles and boundaries • Reset the decision making culture • Focus on great conflict resolution • Learn to deal with members who violate the charter. • Timely feedback on non productive behaviours	• Focus on conflict mangement • Address skills gaps • Introduce shared decision making to avoid 'old lion' effect • Address destructive and unethical behavoiur head on • Be supportive and encourage individuals to focus on team goals, over individuality

NORMING

Observations	Feelings	Needs	Your Job
• Conflict is either avoided to keep the peace or managed effectively inside the team • Processes are established and followed naturally without having to reconfirm • Shared problem solving • Confident energy that is balanced • Acceptance of different opinions that are leveraged not dismissed	• General feeling of safety • Confidence • Trust feels higher • Members demonstrate a willingness to help without hesitation • Seniors naturally help the more junior members	• Establish team leaders and set decision making process • Encourage input from all members to solve problems	• Provide ongoing encouragement to solve problems without your input • Feedback when things go wrong should be confidence building • Help them learn along the way • Encourage full input for all team members • Celebrate their wins

122

PERFORMING

Observations	Feelings	Needs	Your Job
• Members are flexible and work to deliver results and value • Sense of shared wins and losses • Roles are full established and clear • Self organisation • Less need for conflict resolution • Momentum is achieved with little management	• Commitment is demonstrated, both to outcomes and the other members • Natural high levels of confidence • Genuine and authentic communication styles • Fun, excitement	• Continued focus on collaboration and goals • Measure of output and performance • Continued information giving, and leadership	• Communicate vision, and continue to share team future goals • Focus on feedback and development activities for team members • Continually encourage and create a collaborative environment • Allow the team to make local decisions and support them

About the Author

Nadeen is a seasoned technology team leader and manager with over two decades of experience across retail banking, telecoms and CMS sectors.

She believes that every messy team is fixable. It just takes time, a systematic, but tailored, approach, along with a decent dose of courage. She also believes that the success of any young person today in leading technology teams lies in compassionate coaching and ongoing mentoring on how to navigate the choppy waters.

She hopes this introduction to messy teams will provide actionable lessons for young team leaders, that will transform them from a deer in the headlights to a confident and in-control individual, worthy of the team leader role.

URGENT PLEA!

Thank You For Reading My Book!

I really appreciate all of your feedback and
I love hearing what you have to say.

Please take two minutes now to leave a helpful review on
Amazon letting me know what you thought of the book:
messyteams.com/review
Thanks so much!

NADEEN

selfpublishing.com

NOW IT'S YOUR TURN

**Discover the EXACT 3-step blueprint you need to become
a bestselling author in as little as 3 months.**

Self-Publishing School helped me, and now I want them to help
you with this FREE resource to begin outlining your book!
Even if you're busy, bad at writing, or don't know where to start,
you CAN write a bestseller and build your best life.
With tools and experience across a variety of niches and professions,
Self-Publishing School is the <u>only</u> resource you need to
take your book to the finish line!

DON'T WAIT
Say "YES" to becoming a bestseller:
https://selfpublishing.com/friend/

Follow the steps on the page to get a FREE resource to
get started on your book and unlock a discount to get
started with SelfPublishing.com

Printed in Great Britain
by Amazon